Andrew Lloyd Webber®
Classics

TITLE	PAGE	TRACK WITH MELODY CUE	TRACK ACCOMPANIMENT ONLY
The Phantom Of The Opera from *The Phantom Of The Opera*	2	1	2
Don't Cry For Me Argentina from *Evita*	4	3	4
Close Every Door from *Joseph And The Amazing Technicolor® Dreamcoat*	5	5	6
As If We Never Said Goodbye from *Sunset Boulevard*	6	7	8
Everything's Alright from *Jesus Christ Superstar*	7	9	10
Gus: The Theatre Cat from *Cats*	8	11	12
Unexpected Song from *Song & Dance*	10	13	14
The Music Of The Night from *The Phantom Of The Opera*	11	15	16
Love Changes Everything from *Aspects Of Love*	12	17	18
Whistle Down The Wind from *Whistle Down The Wind*	13	19	20
Our Kind Of Love from *The Beautiful Game*	14	21	22
Go Go Go Joseph from *Joseph And The Amazing Technicolor® Dreamcoat*	15	23	24
B♭ *Tuning Notes*		25	

How To Use The CD Accompaniment:
A melody cue appears on the right channel only. If your CD player has a balance adjustment, you can adjust the volume of the melody by turning down the right channel.

ISBN 0-634-06154-2

HAL•LEONARD®
CORPORATION
7777 W. BLUEMOUND RD. P.O. BOX 13819 MILWAUKEE, WI 53213

Visit Hal Leonard Online at
www.halleonard.com

THE PHANTOM OF THE OPERA
from THE PHANTOM OF THE OPERA

Music by ANDREW LLOYD WEBBER
Lyrics by CHARLES HART
Additional Lyrics by RICHARD STILGOE and MIKE BATT

CLARINET

DON'T CRY FOR ME ARGENTINA

from EVITA

Words by TIM RICE
Music by ANDREW LLOYD WEBBER

CLARINET

CLOSE EVERY DOOR
from JOSEPH AND THE AMAZING TECHNICOLOR® DREAMCOAT

CD

◆**5** : With melody cue
◆**6** : Accompaniment only

Music by ANDREW LLOYD WEBBER
Lyrics by TIM RICE

CLARINET

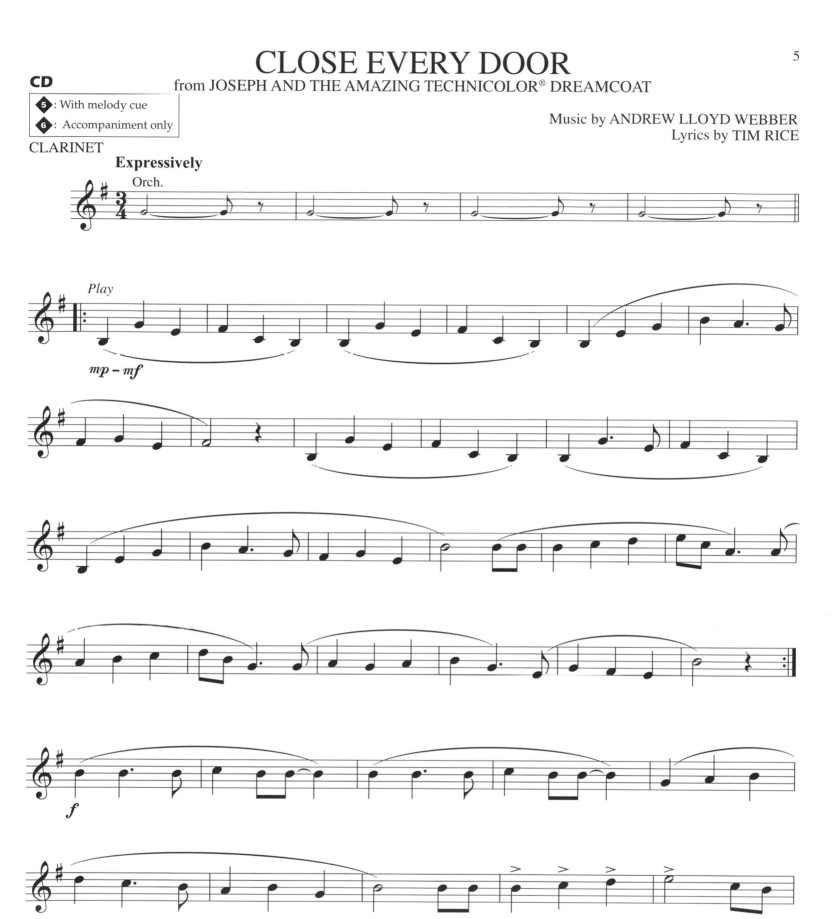

AS IF WE NEVER SAID GOODBYE
from SUNSET BOULEVARD

CD

7 : With melody cue
8 : Accompaniment only

CLARINET

Music by ANDREW LLOYD WEBBER
Lyrics by DON BLACK and CHRISTOPHER HAMPTON,
with contributions by AMY POWERS

EVERYTHING'S ALRIGHT
from JESUS CHRIST SUPERSTAR

Words by TIM RICE
Music by ANDREW LLOYD WEBBER

CD

◆ 9 : With melody cue
◆ 10 : Accompaniment only

CLARINET

GUS: THE THEATRE CAT
from CATS

CD

🎵 11: With melody cue
🎵 12: Accompaniment only

CLARINET

Music by ANDREW LLOYD WEBBER
Text by T.S. ELIOT

Somewhat faster

UNEXPECTED SONG
from SONG & DANCE

Music by ANDREW LLOYD WEBBER
Lyrics by DON BLACK

CD

13: With melody cue
14: Accompaniment only

CLARINET

THE MUSIC OF THE NIGHT
from THE PHANTOM OF THE OPERA

Music by ANDREW LLOYD WEBBER
Lyrics by CHARLES HART
Additional Lyrics by RICHARD STILGOE

CD

15 : With melody cue
16 : Accompaniment only

CLARINET

LOVE CHANGES EVERYTHING
from ASPECTS OF LOVE

Music by ANDREW LLOYD WEBBER
Lyrics by DON BLACK and CHARLES HART

WHISTLE DOWN THE WIND
from WHISTLE DOWN THE WIND

CD

19: With melody cue
20: Accompaniment only

Music by ANDREW LLOYD WEBBER
Lyrics by JIM STEINMAN

Clarinet

OUR KIND OF LOVE
from THE BEAUTIFUL GAME

Music by ANDREW LLOYD WEBBER
Lyrics by BEN ELTON

CD

21 : With melody cue
22 : Accompaniment only

CLARINET

GO GO GO JOSEPH
from JOSEPH AND THE AMAZING TECHNICOLOR® DREAMCOAT

Music by ANDREW LLOYD WEBBER
Lyrics by TIM RICE

CD

23 : With melody cue
24 : Accompaniment only

CLARINET

PLAY MORE OF YOUR FAVORITE SONGS
WITH GREAT INSTRUMENTAL PLAY ALONG PACKS FROM HAL LEONARD

Ballads
Solo arrangements of 12 songs: Bridge Over Troubled Water • Bring Him Home • Candle in the Wind • Don't Cry for Me Argentina • I Don't Know How to Love Him • Imagine • Killing Me Softly with His Song • Nights in White Satin • Wonderful Tonight • more.

00841445	Flute	$10.95
00841446	Clarinet	$10.95
00841447	Alto Sax	$10.95
00841448	Tenor Sax	$10.95
00841449	Trumpet	$10.95
00841450	Trombone	$10.95
00841451	Violin	$10.95

Band Jam
12 band favorites complete with accompaniment CD, including: Born to Be Wild • Get Ready for This • I Got You (I Feel Good) • Rock & Roll – Part II (The Hey Song) • Twist and Shout • We Will Rock You • Wild Thing • Y.M.C.A • and more.

00841232	Flute	$10.95
00841233	Clarinet	$10.95
00841234	Alto Sax	$10.95
00841235	Trumpet	$10.95
00841236	Horn	$10.95
00841237	Trombone	$10.95
00841238	Violin	$10.95

Disney Movie Hits
Now solo instrumentalists can play along with a dozen favorite songs from Disney blockbusters, including: Beauty and the Beast • Circle of Life • Cruella De Vil • Go the Distance • God Help the Outcasts • Kiss the Girl • When She Loved Me • A Whole New World • and more.

00841420	Flute	$12.95
00841421	Clarinet	$12.95
00841422	Alto Sax	$12.95
00841423	Trumpet	$12.95
00841424	French Horn	$12.95
00841425	Trombone/Baritone	$12.95
00841686	Tenor Sax	$12.95
00841687	Oboe	$12.95
00841688	Mallet Percussion	$12.95
00841426	Violin	$12.95
00841427	Viola	$12.95
00841428	Cello	$12.95

FOR MORE INFORMATION, SEE YOUR LOCAL MUSIC DEALER, OR WRITE TO:

HAL•LEONARD CORPORATION
7777 W. BLUEMOUND RD. P.O. BOX 13819 MILWAUKEE, WI 53213

Visit Hal Leonard online at www.halleonard.com

Disney Solos
An exciting collection of 12 solos with full-band accompaniment on CD. Songs include: Be Our Guest • Can You Feel the Love Tonight • Colors of the Wind • Reflection • Under the Sea • You've Got a Friend in Me • Zero to Hero • and more.

00841404	Flute	$12.95
00841405	Clarinet/Tenor Sax	$12.95
00841406	Alto Sax	$12.95
00841407	Horn	$12.95
00841408	Trombone	$12.95
00841409	Trumpet	$12.95
00841410	Violin	$12.95
00841411	Viola	$12.95
00841412	Cello	$12.95
00841506	Oboe	$12.95
00841553	Mallet Percussion	$12.95

Easy Disney Favorites
13 Disney favorites for solo instruments: Bibbidi-Bobbidi-Boo • It's a Small World • Let's Go Fly a Kite • Mickey Mouse March • A Spoonful of Sugar • Toyland March • Winnie the Pooh • The Work Song • Zip-A-Dee-Doo-Dah • and many more.

00841371	Flute	$12.95
00841477	Clarinet	$12.95
00841478	Alto Sax	$12.95
00841479	Trumpet	$12.95
00841480	Trombone	$12.95
00841372	Violin	$12.95
00841481	Viola	$12.95
00841482	Cello/Bass	$12.95

Favorite Movie Themes
13 themes, including: *An American Symphony* from Mr. Holland's Opus • Braveheart • Chariots of Fire • Forrest Gump – Main Title • Theme from *Jurassic Park* • Mission: Impossible Theme • and more.

00841166	Flute	$10.95
00841167	Clarinet	$10.95
00841168	Trumpet/Tenor Sax	$10.95
00841169	Alto Sax	$10.95
00841170	Trombone	$10.95
00841171	F Horn	$10.95
00841296	Violin	$10.95

Jazz & Blues
14 songs: Cry Me a River • Fever • Fly Me to the Moon • God Bless' the Child • Harlem Nocturne • Moonglow • A Night in Tunisia • One Note Samba • Satin Doll • Take the "A" Train • Yardbird Suite • and more.

00841438	Flute	$10.95
00841439	Clarinet	$10.95
00841440	Alto Sax	$10.95
00841441	Trumpet	$10.95
00841442	Tenor Sax	$10.95
00841443	Trombone	$10.95
00841444	Violin	$10.95

Lennon and McCartney Solos
11 favorites: All My Loving • Can't Buy Me Love • Eleanor Rigby • The Long and Winding Road • Ticket to Ride • Yesterday • and more.

00841542	Flute	$10.95
00841543	Clarinet	$10.95
00841544	Alto Sax	$10.95
00841545	Tenor Sax	$10.95
00841546	Trumpet	$10.95
00841547	Horn	$10.95
00841548	Trombone	$10.95
00841549	Violin	$10.95
00841625	Viola	$10.95
00841626	Cello	$10.95

Movie & TV Themes
12 favorite themes: A Whole New World • Where Everybody Knows Your Name • Moon River • Theme from Schindler's List • Theme from Star Trek® • You Must Love Me • and more.

00841452	Flute	$10.95
00841453	Clarinet	$10.95
00841454	Alto Sax	$10.95
00841455	Tenor Sax	$10.95
00841456	Trumpet	$10.95
00841457	Trombone	$10.95
00841458	Violin	$10.95

Sound of Music
9 songs: Climb Ev'ry Mountain • Do-Re-Mi • Edelweiss • The Lonely Goatherd • Maria • My Favorite Things • Sixteen Going on Seventeen • So Long, Farewell • The Sound of Music.

00841582	Flute	$10.95
00841583	Clarinet	$10.95
00841584	Alto Sax	$10.95
00841585	Tenor Sax	$10.95
00841586	Trumpet	$10.95
00841587	Horn	$10.95
00841588	Trombone	$10.95
00841589	Violin	$10.95
00841590	Viola	$10.95
00841591	Cello	$10.95

Worship Solos
11 top worship songs: Come, Now Is the Time to Worship • Draw Me Close • Firm Foundation • I Could Sing of Your Love Forever • Open the Eyes of My Heart • Shout to the North • and more.

00841836	Flute	$12.95
00841837	Oboe	$12.95
00841838	Clarinet	$12.95
00841839	Alto Sax	$12.95
00841840	Tenor Sax	$12.95
00841841	Trumpet	$12.95
00841842	Horn	$12.95
00841843	Trombone	$12.95
00841844	Violin	$12.95
00841845	Viola	$12.95
00841846	Cello	$12.95